Practical Design & Technology
CAD/CAM Constructions

Steven Atkin & Richard Beeden

Heinemann
LIBRARY

H www.heinemann.co.uk/library

Visit our website to find out more information about **Heinemann Library** books.

To order:

☎ Phone 44 (0) 1865 888066

📄 Send a fax to 44 (0) 1865 314091

💻 Visit the Heinemann Bookshop at www.heinemann.co.uk/library to browse our catalogue and order online.

First published in Great Britain by Heinemann Library, Halley Court, Jordan Hill, Oxford OX2 8EJ, part of Harcourt Education. Heinemann is a registered trademark of Harcourt Education Ltd.

Editorial: Andrew Farrow, Lucy Thunder and Helen Cox
Design: David Poole and Paul Myerscough
Illustrations: Geoff Ward
Picture Research: Catherine Bevan and Rebecca Sodergren
Production: Séverine Ribierre

Originated by Ambassador Litho Ltd
Printed in Hong Kong, China by Wing King Tong

ISBN 0 431 17582 9
07 06 05 04 03
10 9 8 7 6 5 4 3 2 1

British Library Cataloguing in Publication Data
Atkin, Steven and Beeden, Richard
CAD/CAM Constructions
620'.0042'0285
A full catalogue record for this book is available from the British Library.

Acknowledgements
The publishers would like to thank the following for permission to reproduce photographs: AME Product Development Solutions pp**5**, **22**, **23**, **24a**, **24b**, **25a**, **25b**; Gareth Boden pp**7**, **19**, **20**, **26a**, **26b**, **29a**, **29b**, **29c**, **29d**, **30a**, **33a**, **33b**, **33c**, **35a**, **37a**, **37b**, **37c**, **39a**, **40a**, **40b**, **41a**, **41b**; Getty Images p**14**; Suregrave (UK) Ltd p**13d**; Techsoft UK Ltd pp**12a**, **13a**, **13b**, **13c**; Tudor Photography pp**9a**, **9b**, **10**, **11**, **16**, **30b**, **32**, **34b**, **34a**, **36**, **38**, **42**, **43**, **44**, **45**.

Cover photograph of a screen grab of the FOAP project and the Superbright light, reproduced with permission of Richard Beeden and Gareth Boden.

The publishers would like to thank Andy Bird for his assistance in the preparation of this book, and the staff and pupils of both Hope Valley College, Derbyshire and Wales High School, Rotherham. Also, thanks to the following companies for their assistance: AME Product Development Solutions, Economatics (Education) Ltd, Hindleys Ltd, Rapid Electronics Ltd, Roland Digital Group, Suregrave (UK) Limited, Techsoft UK Ltd.

Every effort has been made to contact copyright holders of any material reproduced in this book. Any omissions will be rectified in subsequent printings if notice is given to the publishers.

21136658W

Contents

Any words appearing in the text in bold, **like this,** are explained in the Glossary.

Introduction to CAD/CAM

Computer Aided Design (CAD) and Computer Aided Manufacture (CAM) are processes that are becoming very important to industry all over the world. CAD/CAM really means the process of designing and making things using computers and computer-controlled machines. This book provides an interesting insight to the individual processes of CAD and CAM, looking at the equipment and software that is commonly used in industry and schools.

The way in which products are designed and manufactured using CAD and CAM is different to more traditional methods of manufacture.

We have broken down the whole procedure into easy to understand stages to enable you to design and make your own products. There are four detailed examples of CAD/CAM projects in the book that you can use as starting points for your products, as well as four further project ideas.

The advantages of CAD/CAM

CAD and CAM should be thought of as two separate operations, with different skills and equipment required for each. The reasons why CAD and CAM are such successful processes today are:

- The length of time required for a product to be designed and a **prototype** produced is generally quicker than more traditional methods. Any changes that are needed can be made before the actual manufacturing process starts and before too much money has been spent.

- The whole process reduces the 'time to market'. This means that products are less likely to fail because the market changes or because a competitor launches its product first.

- CAM machines can produce a working prototype using a wide range of materials such as foam board, MDF (medium density fibreboard), metals and special plastics that can be made to look like other materials, saving time and money.

- CAD can be used to test products, reducing risk in real situations. An example of this is where a **computer model** is **rendered** and viewed from all angles to ensure that it looks good and is **proportionally** correct.

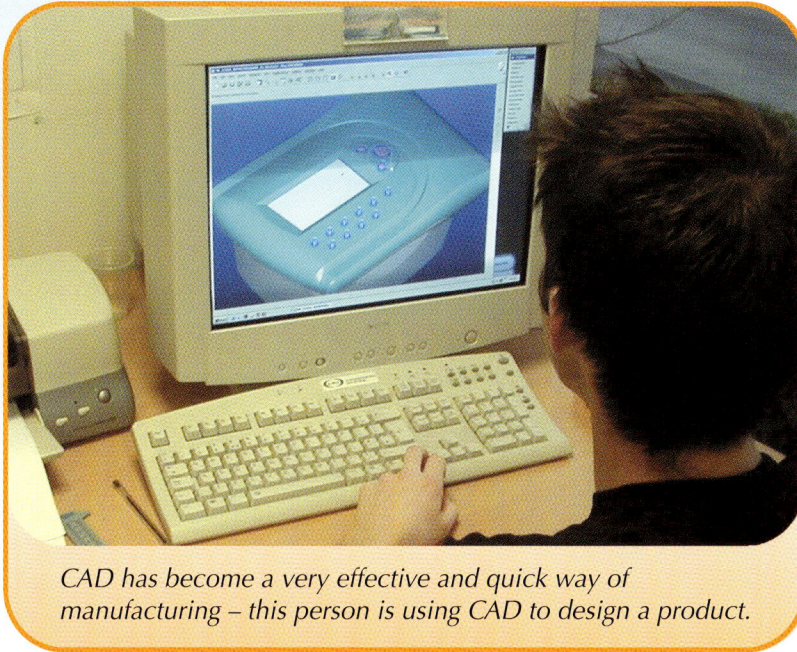

CAD has become a very effective and quick way of manufacturing – this person is using CAD to design a product.

Computer Aided Design

CAD is the process of designing or putting a design onto a computer. CAD allows designers to carry out a number of particular tasks:

- draw objects to scale
- draw lines, curves and circles accurately
- create 2-dimensional (2D) and 3-dimensional (3D) objects
- move objects around on the screen
- assemble different parts to form complete products
- drawings can be flipped, stretched, rotated, copied and rendered.

Computer Aided Manufacture

CAM is the process of making something on a machine that is controlled by a computer. These machines are often called **CNC** machines, which stands for Computer Numeric Control. This is because the drawings that are produced on the CAD program are converted into numbers for the CAM machine to understand. These numbers refer to the direction and distance that the machine will have to move in order to manufacture the product. There are many different types of CAM machines. Some CAM machines are based on more traditional machines such as:

- **milling machines**
- **lathes**
- **plotters**.

Some CAM machines can produce objects using modern production methods, such as:

- **stereolithography**
- 3D printing
- **laser etching**.

The design process

The task of designing and making something can be very complicated. The designer needs to think about a wide range of different things, from the materials that could be used to the requirements of the **consumer**. The whole activity is often described as the design process. The design process is a framework for designing and making that is used by designers all over the world to design and manufacture a wide range of products. This book will look at the design process for designing and making CAD/CAM products, that is, products that are designed and manufactured using computers and computer-operated machines. The design process has nine stages and is as follows:

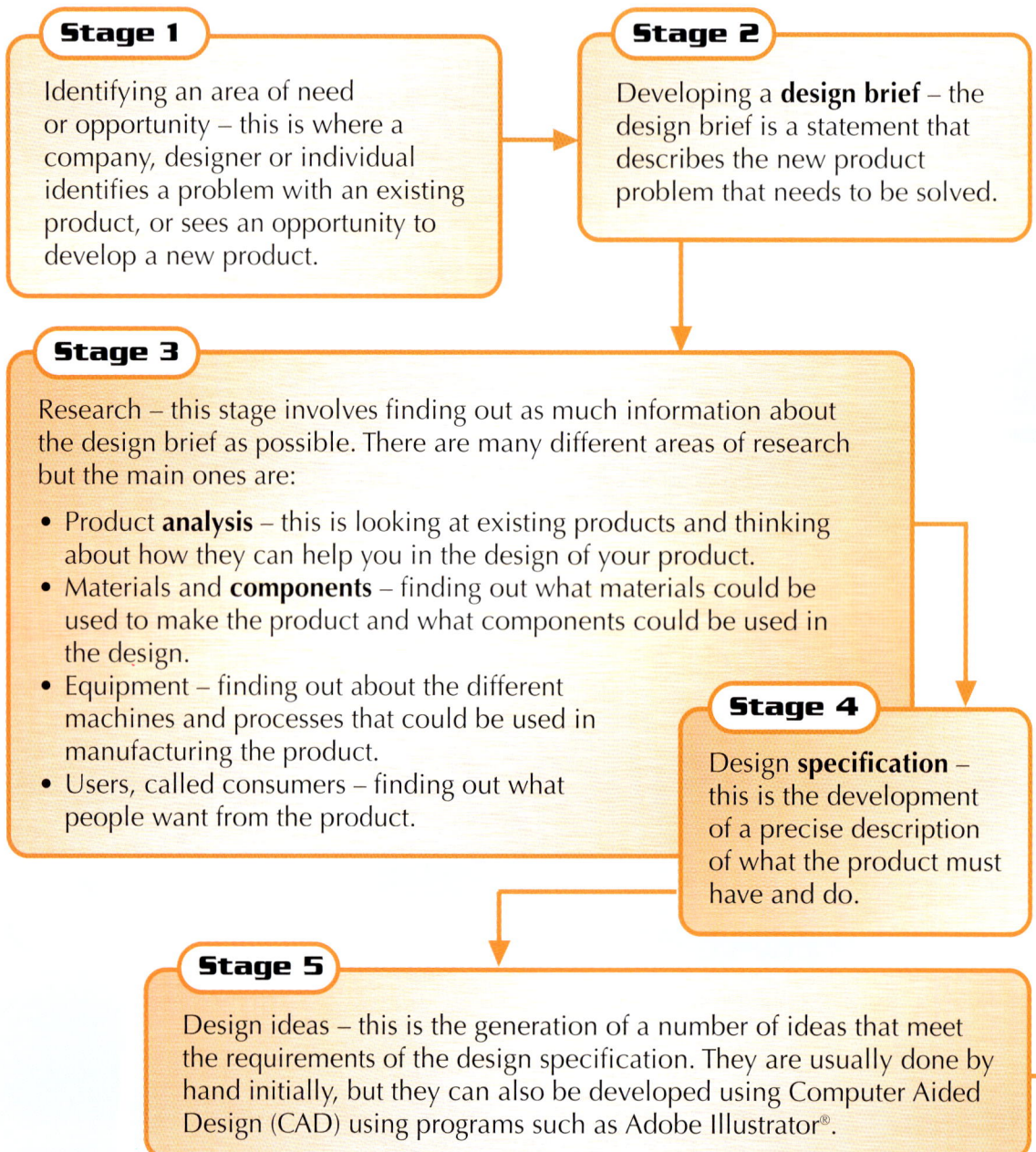

Stage 1

Identifying an area of need or opportunity – this is where a company, designer or individual identifies a problem with an existing product, or sees an opportunity to develop a new product.

Stage 2

Developing a **design brief** – the design brief is a statement that describes the new product problem that needs to be solved.

Stage 3

Research – this stage involves finding out as much information about the design brief as possible. There are many different areas of research but the main ones are:

- Product **analysis** – this is looking at existing products and thinking about how they can help you in the design of your product.
- Materials and **components** – finding out what materials could be used to make the product and what components could be used in the design.
- Equipment – finding out about the different machines and processes that could be used in manufacturing the product.
- Users, called consumers – finding out what people want from the product.

Stage 4

Design **specification** – this is the development of a precise description of what the product must have and do.

Stage 5

Design ideas – this is the generation of a number of ideas that meet the requirements of the design specification. They are usually done by hand initially, but they can also be developed using Computer Aided Design (CAD) using programs such as Adobe Illustrator®.

Stage 6

Product development – this is the process of getting from a number of design ideas to the point, called the design solution, at which you are ready to manufacture the first version of the product (the **prototype**). This stage involves **modelling** different ways of making the product, and the production of working drawings and manufacturing instructions. 3D CAD software such as Pro/Desktop® is often used at this stage.

Stage 7

Planning – this is the accurate planning of how you are going to make the final product. It is often done in the form of a **flowchart**, with different symbols used to represent different stages of the making process.

Stage 8

Manufacturing – this is making your product.

Stage 9

Testing and **evaluation** – it is very important that the product is fully tested to check that it meets the requirements of the design specification. Evaluating means thinking about how well the project has gone. It can be broken down into three main questions:

1 What have I done well?
2 What could I have done better?
3 How could I improve the finished product?

! Health and safety

Health and safety rules for using CAD/CAM machinery

- Always ensure that the machine is programmed correctly, making sure that the machine knows the exact size and type of material that is being cut.
- All CAD/CAM machines that use revolving cutters have guards that must be in place in order for machining to begin. Never try to **override** this facility. Always be extremely careful when handling the machine cutting tools.
- Make sure that you know where the emergency stop button is located on a CAM machine so that you can end an unsuccessful run quickly.
- If in any doubt, ask an adult or teacher who understands how the machine works to help you.

Using cutting boards and knifes

- Use a cutting board at all times.
- Always hold a knife blade like a pencil.
- Use a safety ruler to cut straight lines.

The emergency stop button on a CAM machine.

Research: Product analysis

Research means finding information that will help you to design and manufacture your project. This research can be carried out in lots of different ways, and it is a very important part of the design process. There are a variety of sources of information available for research, which include:

- books, magazines and catalogues
- the Internet
- shops
- CD-Roms
- television

Research can also be carried out using testing and experimentation. For example, before deciding on what material is best suited to a particular product, you might test its properties by carrying out a **controlled experiment**. As there are so many different sources of information it is important that you decide what you want to know before you begin the process of gathering research for your project. In the following pages we are going to look at four areas of research that will help you to design and make things using CAD/CAM:

1 product **analysis**
2 materials and **components**
3 equipment
4 users.

Product analysis

Product analysis is a very important part of the design process. It means looking at existing products and working out:

- the key features of the product
- how it is manufactured
- the materials that it is made out of
- how it works
- how well it works.

The first stage of product analysis is to find examples of products that are similar to the one that you are designing. This does not mean that you must find a product that is exactly the same as the one that you are working on. It is more likely that you will identify particular features of other products that you like. You can then think about how these features could be used to improve your design.

A ballpoint pen

Here we are going to analyse a product that will
contribute to the animal pen project that can be found
later in this book. The product is the Bic® Crystal
ballpoint pen, which has been in production since 1950.
It is an excellent example of good design:

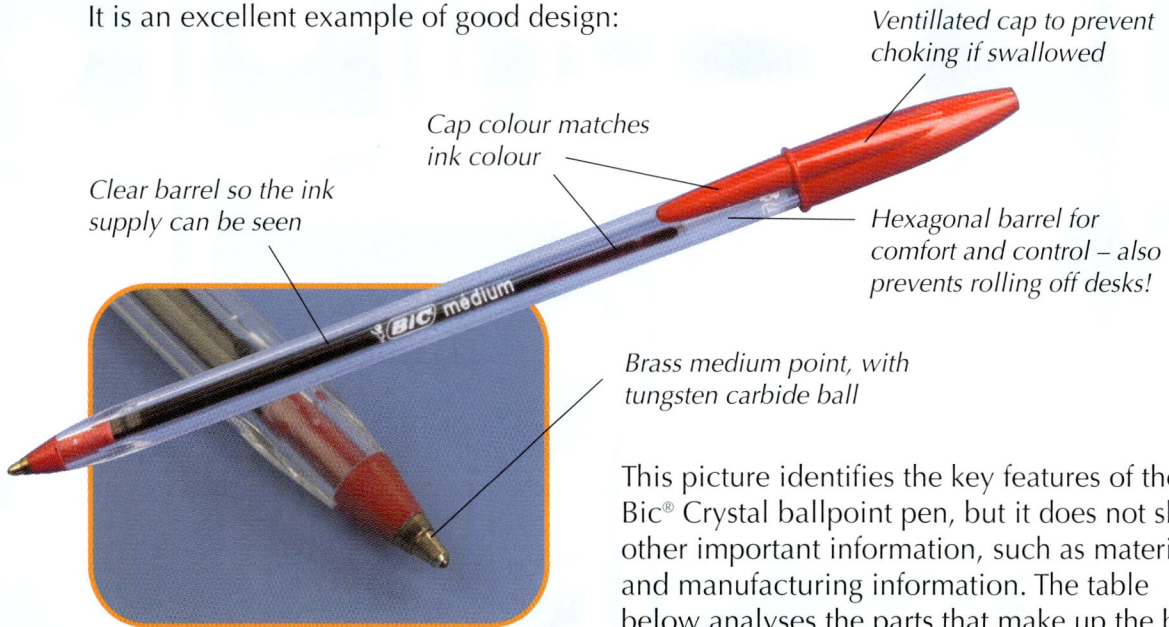

*Ventillated cap to prevent
choking if swallowed*

*Cap colour matches
ink colour*

*Clear barrel so the ink
supply can be seen*

*Hexagonal barrel for
comfort and control – also
prevents rolling off desks!*

*Brass medium point, with
tungsten carbide ball*

This picture identifies the key features of the
Bic® Crystal ballpoint pen, but it does not show
other important information, such as materials
and manufacturing information. The table
below analyses the parts that make up the biro:

Product	Bic® Crystal ballpoint pen			
Manufacturer	Bic			
Part of pen	**Analysis of part**			
	Material	**Manufacturing process**	**Aesthetics (0–3)**	**Effectiveness (0–3)**
Barrel	Polystyrene	**Injection moulded**	2	3
Barrel cap	Polypropylene	Injection moulded	1	3
Lid	Polypropylene	Injection moulded	1	3
Ink cartridge	Polystyrene	Injection moulded	1	3
Ballpoint	Brass/tungsten carbide	**Fabrication**	1	3
Product rating	0 – Poor 1 – Average 2 – Good 3 – Excellent			

Here the pen is rated as excellent overall mainly because of the
effectiveness of the parts rather than their **aesthetics**. You can use this type of
table to analyse any product, though it can be difficult to find out how a
product is made. You might have to use company Internet sites or write a
letter to find out specific information about a product.

Research: Materials and components

Computer Aided Manufacturing has the capability to **machine** the majority of materials that are available to designers today. The most commonly machined materials fall into two groups:

- Thermoplastics – these are plastics that can melt and return to their original state.

- **Non-ferrous metals** – these are metals that do not contain iron.

The table below shows the materials and **components** that can be used on the majority of CAD/CAM machines.

Material	Properties	Cost	Use
Plastics			
Expanded foam ('Foamex')	Sheet material in various colours. Available in different thicknesses. The most common thicknesses for CAD/CAM applications are 3 mm – 6 mm. It has low friction with the machine bit and can be machined at 40 mm/second.	Medium	All 2D CAD/CAM projects requiring material that is 3 mm or more thick.
Polystyrene	Often used for **vacuum forming**. This can melt onto the cutter during machining. It is useful for thin projects (< 3 mm) and is available in a wide range of colours.	Low	Low quality, flexible CAD/CAM products.
Acrylic	Hard, durable material that is available in a range of colours as well as transparent. It is hard wearing on machine cutters and scratches easily.	High	High quality, ornamental CAD/CAM products.
Metals			
Aluminium	A light, soft material that is easy to machine using CAD/CAM. Can be found in all shapes and sizes, but is difficult to join.	Medium	Suitable for a range of CAD/CAM projects, though it must be securely fastened to the machine bed.

Material	Properties	Cost	Use
Other			
PCB board	Copper-faced cardboard is best used for CAD/CAM production – it wears less on the machine cutter.	High	Used to manufacture printed circuit boards (PCBs) for electric circuits.
TS foam	Low and medium density foam that comes in sheets up to 45 mm thick.	High	3D CAD/CAM manufacture of moulds and **prototypes**.
Medium density fibreboard (MDF)	Made from compressed wood particles that are bonded together. It has no grain and can therefore be cut in all directions.	Medium	Suitable for 2D and 3D applications.
Modelling wax	Medium density material.	High	High quality 3D CAD/CAM prototyping.
Neoprene	Foam sheets available in a wide range of colours. Sheets also available with a textured surface.	Low	Can be applied to sheet surfaces using double-sided tape to enhance the look and feel of CAD/CAM products.
Plastazote	Similar to Neoprene, available in sheets up to 10 mm thick.	Low	Plastazote can be vacuum formed. It can also be used as a decorative material.
Components			
Plastic sucker	Can be used to fasten objects to smooth surfaces.	Low	Used for products such as toothbrush holders, bird-feeders, toys.
Joggly eyes	Available in a range of sizes up to 50 mm.	Low	Enhance the appearance of faces on products.
Key ring	Metal ring	Low	Attaching keys to CAD/CAM products.

Some of the plastics that can be used on CAD/CAM machines.

Research: CAD/CAM equipment

Computer Aided Design

There are many different CAD packages available to suit a wide range of tasks. CAD is increasingly taking over from more traditional methods of drawing (although sketching ideas is still necessary for all projects) because:

- drawings can be developed more quickly than by using traditional methods
- designs can be changed and developed easily and quickly
- the product can be shown on screen in different formats, materials and colours – this is known as solid **modelling**
- work can be saved and changed or adapted at a later date
- more than one designer can work on the same project at the same time from different places using the Internet
- it is easier to visualize what the final product will look like
- manufacture can be simulated and any problems identified and changed.

The table below shows the properties of two common CAD packages found in schools, colleges and some design companies today:

CAD program	Key features	Output
Techsoft 2D Design Tools® 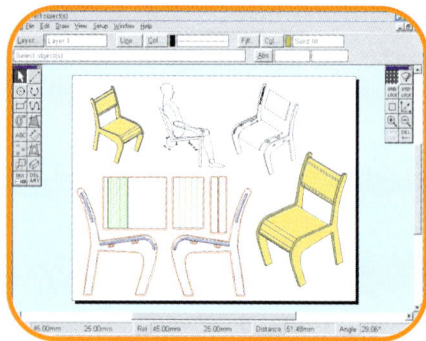	Allows designer to draw using a wide range of graphical tools.	Can **output** to a wide range of CAM machines. Projects found in this book that are designed using this software include: • Animal pen • Superbright light • Toothbrush holder • The mini projects.
Pro/Desktop® 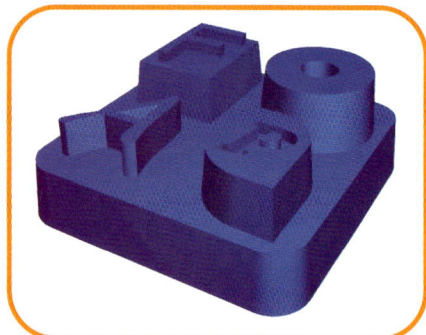	A solid **modelling** program. Pro/Desktop allows designer to draw 3D shapes very accurately.	Outputs drawings and 3D products. The Funky soap is designed and manufactured using this software.

Computer Aided Manufacture

The advantages of using Computer Aided Manufacture over traditional human operated machines include:

- products can be manufactured quickly and accurately, directly from the computer
- the machines can make many copies of a product to exactly the same standard, without any intervention from people
- the machines can be used to make a wide variety of different shapes using the same cutting tool.

Key features of the most common CAM machines found in schools today can be seen in the table below.

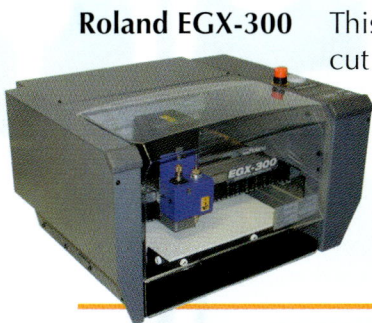

CAM machine	Key features	Output
Roland EGX-300	This machine will cut and engrave plastics and **non-ferrous metals**.	Examples of products in this book that have been manufactured using this machine include: • Animal pen • Toothbrush holder • Superbright light • The mini projects.
Roland Modela MDX-20	This machine is capable of scanning and **milling**, and can be used for cutting 3D shapes.	The Funky soap project in this book was manufactured using this machine.
Roland CX-24	Cuts sticky-backed vinyl and card.	Can be used to cut signs for boxes.
Suregrave Wizzard DT	Cuts and engraves plastics and non-ferrous metals.	

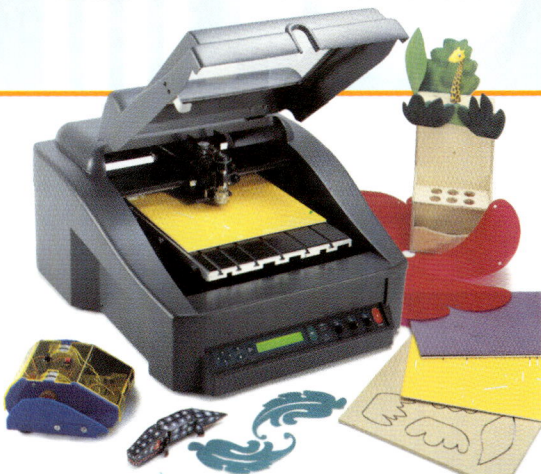

Research: Users

Collecting information about what people want from a particular product is a very important area of research. This information can be gathered in two ways:

1 Personal interview

Interviewing people individually is an excellent method of gathering specific information in detail.

2 Questionnaires

A questionnaire is a form with a number of questions that relate to a product. People fill in the form and return the answers to the designer. The difficult part is writing clear, accurate and easily understood questions. Once the questions have been written the questionnaire can be distributed to people in the **target market**, and later collected and **analysed**.

A market researcher questioning members of the target market.

Both of these methods are effective in gathering information from people, and can of course be used together. In this section we are going to look at how to develop a questionnaire that could be distributed to potential users of a CAD/CAM product. These might be people at school or friends and relatives.

Questionnaires

There are three stages to gathering research through the use of a questionnaire:

1 designing the form and writing the questions
2 distributing and collecting the questionnaire
3 analysing the data.

Designing and writing the questionnaire

The questionnaire must be clearly titled and have precise instructions about what people must do. For example, are you going to use tick-boxes or provide spaces for people to write answers? It is always easier to provide boxes for people to tick.

If you are going to ask people how much they like something, give a scale: for example 1 = poor, 2 = average, 3 = good.

Part of a questionnaire for the Funky soap project on pages 38–41 could look something like the example opposite.

FUNKY SOAP QUESTIONNAIRE

Please return by: _31st March_

Please tick the boxes to answer the following questions.

What is your age?

☐ 5–10 yrs ☑ 11–15 yrs ☐ 15–20 yrs ☐ 20+ yrs

What is your gender?

☐ Male ☑ Female

Tick the box next to the colour you like the most:

☐ Red ☐ Blue ☑ Purple ☐ Gold ☐ Green

Tick the boxes of the scents that you like:

☐ Vanilla ☐ Peach ☐ Strawberry ☑ Lavender ☐ Chocolate

Where do you use soap products?

☑ Bathroom ☑ Kitchen ☐ Garage ☐ Sport ☐ Travel

Distributing and collecting the questionnaire

Try to distribute the questionnaire to the type of people that you are designing the product for and make sure that a record is kept of who has one. You should try to get a variety of different users in order to get a balanced opinion.

Analysis

It is very important that the information collected is analysed accurately. A good way of displaying data visually is by using charts and graphs. To do this you need to have recorded the numbers of people who selected each answer. You also need a software package that will display data graphically, such as Microsoft Excel®.

The information you get from users can help you to decide upon some of the key features of the product. For example, you might want to make your Funky soap smell of strawberry if most people indicate they like that best.

Consumers' favourite scents

10%   15%
15%
25%
35%

☐ Vanilla   ☐ Lavender   ☐ Strawberry
☐ Peach   ☐ Chocolate

An example of displaying the data from the Funky soap scent question.

Design specifications explained

A design **specification** describes in simple, specific sentences what you intend your product to be like and what you hope it will do. It is often separated into a user specification (what it must do to satisfy the people who want it) and a manufacturing specification (how it will be made and to what quality). Specifications set criteria that the product must meet (see the box below). When you **evaluate** your project you will need to refer to the specification to see if your product meets the points in the original specification.

The Mini, first produced in 1959, is an example of a successful design that has lasted for decades. The companies that have manufactured it, such as Rover and BMW, will have created extensive and detailed design specifications for each new model.

User specifications

A user specification is a list of things, called statements or **criteria**, that your product must have or do in order to satisfy the people who will buy it or use it. It should include:

- what the product should do
- its size
- its colour
- its texture
- health and safety factors – the product must not cause its users any harm whilst in use
- how it will be packaged
- instructions – are you going to supply instructions with the product, and if so where will they be?
- how much the product will cost to manufacture.

Manufacturing specifications

This is a list of statements, or criteria, detailing how the product should be made. It should include:

- the materials to be used
- the CAD software required
- the type of CAM equipment needed
- the **tolerance**, or accuracy level, required of the finished product
- how long it will take to make
- how it will be tested.

What type of statement?

Specification statements can be fixed, semi-fixed or open in nature. An example of each would be:

- open statement – My product can be any colour.

- semi-fixed statement – My product will be a bright primary colour.

- fixed statement – My product will be the colour red.

A design specification for a ballpoint pen might look like this:

WONDER-WRITER

User specification:

1. The pen should write using blue, black or red ink.
2. The pen should feel comfortable in the hands of young and old users.
3. The barrel should have a smooth, clean texture.
4. It should have a ventilated lid to ensure that if the lid is swallowed it will not block a person's airways.
5. The lid must have a means of fastening the pen to clothing.
6. The barrel of the pen should be clear so that the amount of ink remaining can be seen.

Manufacturing specification:

1. The barrel will be manufactured out of polystyrene.
2. The cap and fittings will be manufactured out of polypropylene.
3. The plastic parts will be injection moulded.
4. The pen will have a tolerance of 0.1 mm.
5. The pen will take 50 minutes to make.
6. The pen will be tested on different kinds of paper before it is released for sale.

Designing for manufacture

Once you have carried out all the appropriate research and written a design **specification**, you are ready to start to design your product. It can be difficult to draw ideas for a product when faced with a blank piece of paper. It is often useful to produce a bubble diagram representing your design specification and other thoughts that could help the design process:

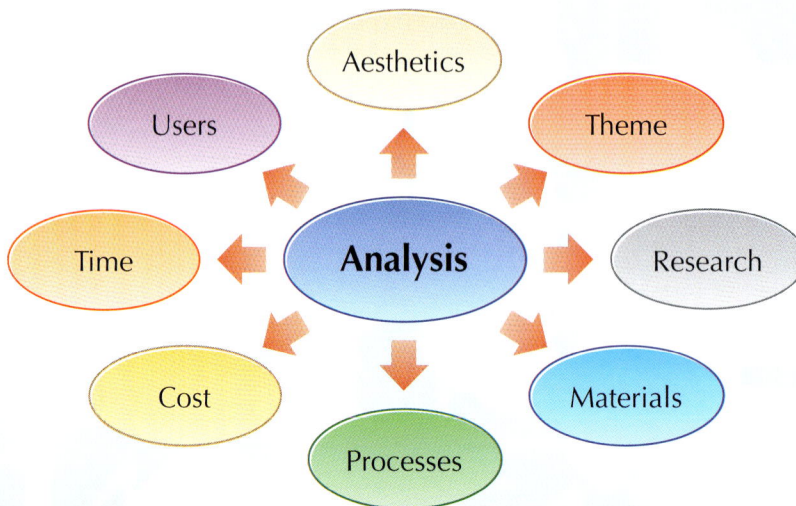

Themes

A bubble diagram could contain a brief reminder of all of the research that has been carried out as well as some ideas for themes. Themes are a very useful way of stimulating design ideas. There are many different themes that you could use, and they may represent a particular interest of the designer. Here are some themes that you might like to consider in your work:

Nature: fish, birds, flowers, leaves, elephants, tigers, weather, dolphins

Popular culture: television programmes, popular music, art and artists, dancing, skateboarding, magazines

Sport: football, tennis, cricket, rugby, hockey, motor racing, cycling, swimming, netball, basketball, gymnastics, martial arts.

A design solution

Using the bubble diagram as a starting point, initial design ideas should:

- be drawn using pencils, to produce freehand sketches
- have materials and features labelled clearly
- use colour where necessary.

Once a range of design ideas has been created, a final design solution should be developed using appropriate drawing equipment (pens). This could simply be your favourite design idea or you could develop a combination of different ideas into a single design.

Design development

The final design solution should then be taken to the CAD stage using a CAD package. Sometimes the design solution cannot be taken to the CAD stage because it will not be appropriate for the manufacturing process chosen or available. In this case, some minor changes will need to be made so that the design can be manufactured. This is known as design development.

Once your design solution has been successfully entered onto the CAD program, the material should be attached securely to the machine bed. The product can then be manufactured and assembled.

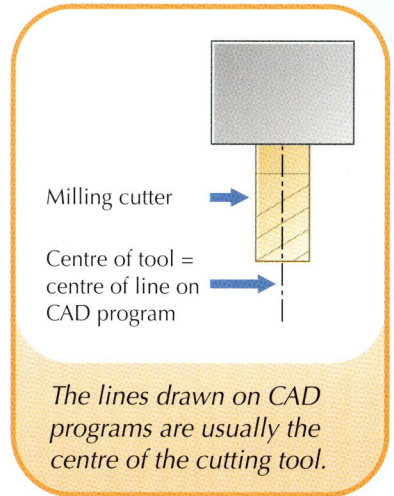

Milling cutter

Centre of tool = centre of line on CAD program

The lines drawn on CAD programs are usually the centre of the cutting tool.

Using CAD/CAM software

Your design solution must take into account the features of the CAD software you are using and the computer-operated machine that is going to be used to manufacture the product. For instance, in most CAD programs, the lines that you draw on screen represent the centre of the machine-cutting tool. This tool is often between 1 mm and 3 mm in diameter, so the line that you see on screen will actually become a lot wider when it is cut. This problem is often solved by the use of **contouring**.

It is also possible to use special features when designing for CAD/CAM:

• The cutter can be programmed to cut to different depths. This means that some shapes or features can be engraved onto the product using either the original **milling** cutter or a dedicated engraving tool. Such features should be marked on the design solution using a coloured pencil.
• In 3D CAD/CAM, the tool moves in three directions, so more complex shapes can be manufactured. However, you must remember that the milling cutter cannot manufacture products with an **undercut**.

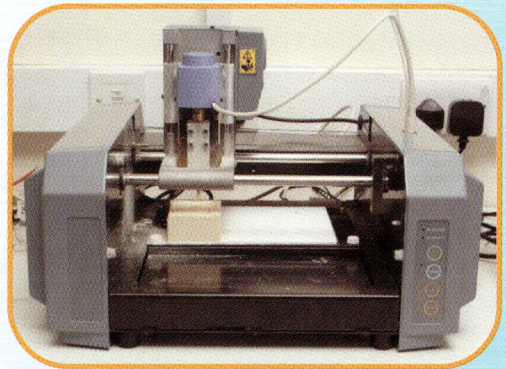

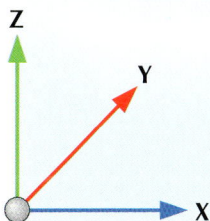

The CAD/CAM machine moves in three directions, as shown above.

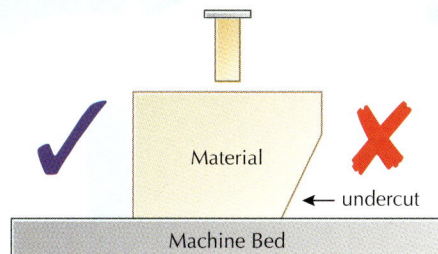

Material

undercut

Machine Bed

Remember when you are working with the milling cutter that it cannot do undercuts.

Evaluation

The purpose of **evaluation** is to improve on what you have done before. Evaluation is something you do every day, probably without even realizing it! For example, you may be evaluating what shoes to buy or food to eat. Your decision will be based on a number of **criteria**. These criteria are similar to those in your design **specification**.

Evaluation is a continual process. Whilst you are designing and making you should also constantly evaluate, and change if necessary, your product.

Evaluating can be more interesting and fun if you discuss your products with a friend.

How to do a final evaluation

A final evaluation is a review of your final product. You will need to decide how successful the final product is. An evaluation can be broken down into three sections.

1 Checking your outcomes against the original specification

Read through your original specification. Now decide if you managed to achieve each specification criteria or point. The specification outlines how you intended your product to turn out, and this may have changed over the course of the design process.

- If you did achieve the specification point, for example that the durability is good, you need to say how this has been achieved.

- If you did not manage to achieve a specification point, say why it was not achieved, or why it was changed. If changes were made, say what they were and how successful they were.

You can write up your assessment of the product as a table, like this:

Specification point	Question	Answer
Colour: My product will be red and white.	Did the product turn out to be red and white?	No, it was clear that just using red and white did not create the right effect. I changed my design and used a range of colours to much better effect. The result was a much more attractive and marketable design.
Size: My product will be small.	Have you kept the product small?	Yes, I managed to keep the product to a hand-held size although it did turn out larger than I had originally intended. This change in size affected the cost of the product but allowed for more detailed design features.

2 Consumer testing

Consumer testing is getting people who might use the product to test it.

- Find out what they think is good about the product (its strengths), and *why* it is good.
- Find out what they think is poor about the product (its weaknesses) and *how* and *why* the product needs to change.

Write up the consumers' comments in a logical way. You may add comments to support other people's views or comments that argue against their views. (Note: This may help you identify strengths and weaknesses in the product to help you with part 3.)

3 Identifying the strengths and weaknesses of your product

- State what you consider to be the strengths of your product and give reasons.
- Then suggest possible modifications and improvements for the weaknesses you have identified.

Industrial case study: AME Product Development Solutions

AME Product Development Solutions is a company that designs products for all kinds of clients. AME specializes in all aspects of product development, such as:

- Research – this includes **market research**, **consumer** research and product forecasting (predicting how well a product will sell).

- Concept design – this is drawing and **modelling** a number of ideas.

- CAD – development of the chosen concept (idea) and initial specification for production. AME uses CAD for two purposes:

  1 Visualization CAD – this is the use of surface modelling with CAD software, such as PTC CDRS®, to show the outside shape, colour and texture of the product.

  2 Detailing CAD – this is the use of solid modelling with CAD software such as PTC Pro/Engineer®, to develop the product so it is ready for manufacture.

- **Rapid prototyping** – rapid prototyping uses advanced technologies such as **stereolithography** to make 3D models quickly and cheaply for pre-production testing.

Some of the team members working at AME.

The AME Development team

AME develops projects using a team of people.

- Project manager – the role of the project manager is to liaise with the client (the organization that **commissions** a project). The project manager must plan the costs and deadlines for the project, and oversee the design process to maintain a consistent standard.

- Industrial designer – the industrial designer comes up with a number of concept solutions (design ideas) to the problem defined by the project manager. The designer works with the client to develop the most appropriate solution.

- CAD operator – the CAD operator uses a range of 3D modelling software to describe the form and create the detail of the product.

- Engineer – the engineer analyses the technical aspects of the product, considering things such as materials, manufacturing processes and product performance.

- Prototyping technician – a **prototyping** technician converts the CAD models into working parts, maintaining high standards of quality throughout.

The design brief

An example of a typical **design brief** that AME gets is the Mitrefinch clocking-in terminal project. Mitrefinch wanted to update their current clocking-in terminal. This is a device that allows people to log what time they start and end their working day. It was hoped that the new product would provide businesses with an extended range of services for employees' time management. In addition Mitrefinch wanted the new product to be easier to maintain on site and to blend in well with offices and hotel lobbies.

The design process

1 Project origination

The project commenced with a creative 'workshop' between AME designers and Mitrefinch staff. The aims of this meeting were to:

- gather information about the company and its products
- think about potential ideas for the project.

2 Concept design ideas

The designers then created three different ideas for the product by hand. These were further developed using software such as Adobe Illustrator®. Simple computer models were created, which were used to make **CNC** models of the outside shape of each design. These were presented to the client for approval (see page 24).

Concept design ideas shown in Adobe Illustrator®.

3 Design development

A design concept was chosen, and was further developed according to suggestions made by Mitrefinch (the client). Manufacturing detail was added to the original CAD model and other fixtures and fittings were specified. It was very important that all of the **components**, including circuit boards, power packs, LCD screen and keyboard, fitted into the casing.

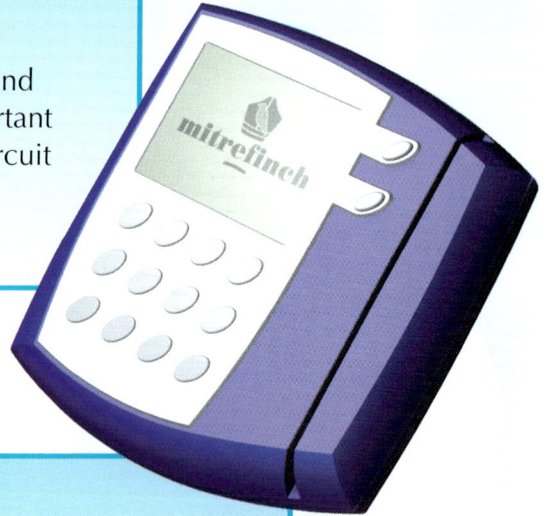

The grey coloured **models** shown are high density foam **outputs** from the CAD images. These models are useful for making judgements about scale, **proportion** and **ergonomics** of the design.

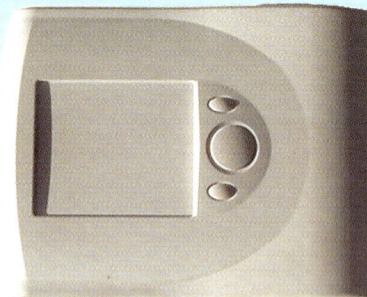

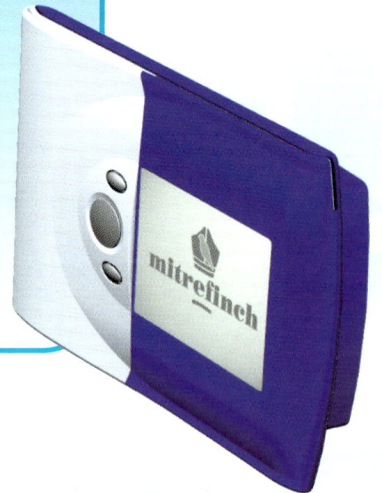

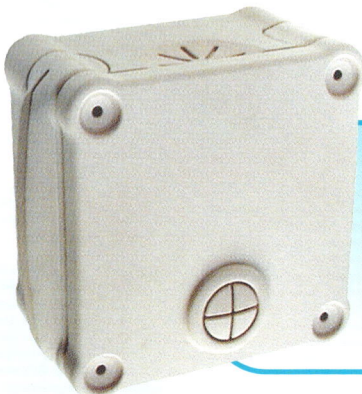

The CAD images are used to display what colours, finishes and materials the product could be.

4 Prototyping

The computer models were then handed over to the prototyping technician. A **stereolithography (SLA)** machine was used to build a physical model of the product. The technicians then finished and textured the model using special paint. This was used to create a silicon rubber mould for **casting** a few parts to test if they would work properly.

This is the soft rubber mould used for the product.

5 The final product

Once the soft mould was found to be successful, a hard, aluminium mould was made that could be used to **injection mould** many hundreds of parts.

The Mitrefinch clocking-in terminal is now in production.

Finally, the finished product – the Mitrefinch clocking-in terminal.

Project 1: The Superbright light

The design brief

A small local company that makes lights has asked you to design and make a hand-held light that could be put onto a key ring or be developed into jewellery. The light must be operated using a **compression switch** and be manufactured using plastics.

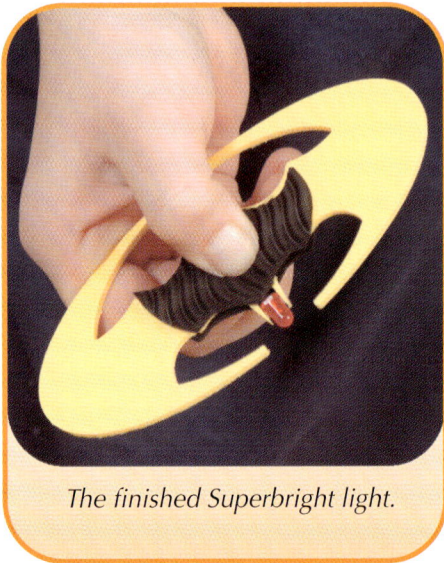

The finished Superbright light.

Product specification

The product **specification** is a list of things your product must be or do:

- the product will use a 5 mm superbright light emitting diode (LED)
- it will be made from Foamex or acrylic plastic
- the compression switch buttons will be made from neoprene and they press onto the LED
- the maximum size of the product is to be 50 mm x 50 mm
- the product will use two small 1.5V battery cells
- the product must be safe for users
- it should last and withstand regular use
- it should be **aesthetically** pleasing (look good).

Before you start to develop your product you should research the existing market. You should identify and analyse any existing products that are similar to the one that you are developing. Think about how you could improve your product and make it better than ones already on the market.

Resources

Materials and components

- double-sided sticky tape
- 3 mm thick plastic – acrylic or Foamex
- 2 x 6.8 mm diameter 1.5V alkaline cell batteries
- 1 x 5 mm superbright LED
- neoprene

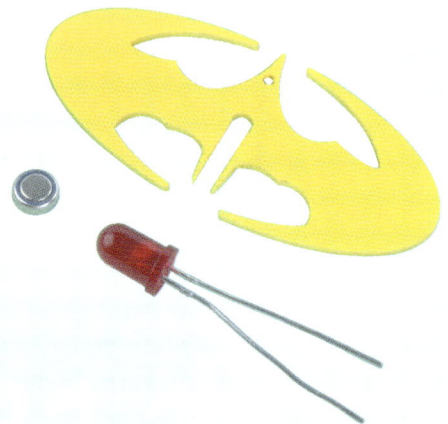

Tools and equipment

- PC/desktop computer
- Computer Aided Design software – Techsoft 2D Design Tools® or equivalent
- Computer Aided Manufacture hardware – **CNC** machine with **milling** and engraving capabilities, like a Roland EGX-300 or a Suregrave Wizzard
- scissors, needle files, abrasive paper, Allen key, ruler

Design ideas

1 Find some themes related to your product. This will help select an area of inspiration for ideas. This can be presented in the form of a bubble diagram.

2 Using a pencil and paper sketch a range of different ideas, for example, animals.

3 Labels parts of your idea if you find it difficult to draw particular features.

4 Use a different coloured pencil to indicate where you want the material to be engraved and cut.

5 Transform your best idea into a silhouetted shape.

6 Produce a circuit diagram for your light.

A design idea for the Superbright light shown on a computer in CAD.

7 Using a CAD package, for example Techsoft 2D Design Tools®, draw your shape onto the computer.

8 Using the CAD software, modify your design idea until you are happy with it.

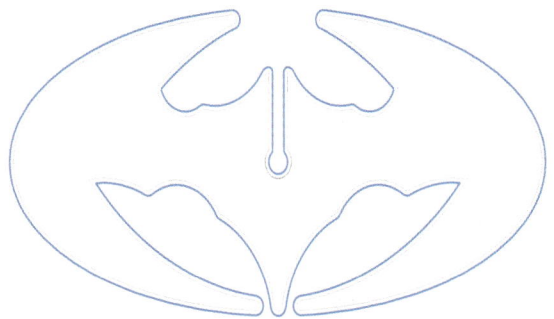

Hints for success

! Keep ideas simple. Some of the best ideas are simple, but still very effective.

! Use **templates** if needed for more complex design details.

! Use the full range of drawing tools on the CAD software to manipulate and change your design. Let the computer do the work.

! Allow the CAM machine to make a number of cutting passes. Do not try to cut through material in one go.

! Make sure the CAM machine cuts at the right speed for the material.

! Take the time to finish your product with files and abrasive paper.

! Take care when making, do not rush!

Action plan

Use the following steps as the basis of an action plan for manufacturing your product:

Action	Resources	Time needed
1 Fix material to the bed of the CAM machine with double-sided tape	• 3 mm Foamex or acrylic plastic sheet • Double-sided sticky tape	10 mins
2 Fix correct cutting tool into CAM machine	• **Milling** or engraving tool • Allen key	3 mins
3 Set CAM machine to ready	• CAM machine	2 mins
4 Load your design into CAD software and select area for cutting	• PC • CAD software	5 mins
5 Set up cutting depths in CAD software	• PC • CAD software	2 mins
6 **Output** design from CAD software to CAM machine	• PC • CAD software • CAM machine	1 min
7 Watch CAM machine cut material and make product	• CAM machine	2 mins
8 Remove cut material from bed	• Ruler	1 min
9 Clean up material with needle files	• Needle files	10 mins
10 Finish material with abrasive paper	• Abrasive paper	10 mins
11 Cut neoprene to size with scissors	• Scissors • Neoprene	10 mins
12 Fix battery cells and LED in place	• 2 x 6.8 mm 1.5V battery cells • 5 mm superbright LED	10 mins
13 Fix neoprene **compression switch** with double-sided sticky tape	• Neoprene compression switch • Double-sided sticky tape	5 mins
14 Test product	• Product	10 mins

7

11

Evaluation

Answer the following questions about your product:

- Am I pleased with my finished product?
- In what ways could I make my product better?
- Did I use my time effectively? In what ways?
- Was my design work of a good standard?
- Could my design work be better?
- What do other people think of my work?
- What parts of the project did I find difficult and why?
- Did I enjoy the project?

12

14

Project 2: Toothbrush holder

The design brief

You have been asked to design and manufacture a toothbrush holder that will be packaged with a toothbrush. The product must appeal to young children. You must consider how the product will be packaged and advertised, as these factors are very important when designing for young people.

Product specification

The product **specification** is a list of things your product must have or do:

- the product should fasten to a bathroom wall using a 21 mm diameter plastic sucker
- the product needs to be manufactured from a waterproof material that can be **machined** using **CNC** technology
- the material can be bent using a line heater
- the product can use pre-manufactured **components** such as joggly eyes
- the product must hold one toothbrush securely, yet allow it to be withdrawn and used with ease
- the product must be packaged to appeal to children.

Before you start building your product you should research the exact dimensions of several different toothbrushes that are made for children. You should also research toothbrush packaging and advertising.

Resources

Materials and components

- 3 mm Foamex or acrylic
- 21 mm plastic sucker
- 120 mm x 90 mm plastic bag
- pre-manufactured joggly eyes
- card

Tools and equipment

- PC/desktop computer
- 2D CAD design software, such as Techsoft 2D Design Tools® or equivalent
- 2 mm **milling** cutter
- engraving cutter

- line heater
- Allen key
- scissors, ruler, needle files
- double-sided sticky tape
- coloured pencils/pens

- CAM hardware – CNC machine with milling and engraving capabilities, like a Roland EGX-300 or a Suregrave Wizzard.

Design ideas

1 Produce a bubble diagram about the design brief. Think of themes that could help you with your design work and the colours that appeal to young people.

2 Your design needs to have a hole where the plastic sucker can be attached. You could bear this in mind when designing and try to make it discreet.

3 Try to produce at least ten ideas for the product, using colour to improve the presentation of your work.

4 Label parts of your ideas if you find it difficult to draw particular features.

5 Use a different coloured pencil to indicate where you want the material to bend.

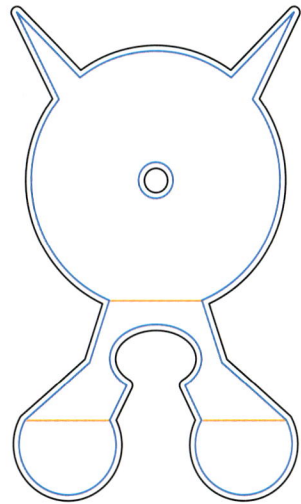

☐ Tool Path 2 mm tool 3 mm depth

☐ Detail drawing

☐ Tool Path 2 mm tool 1.5 mm depth

Material: 3 mm Foamex

Hints for success

! Keep ideas simple. Some of the best ideas are simple, but still very effective.
! Use **templates** if needed for more complex design details.
! Use the full range of drawing tools on the CAD software to manipulate and change your design.
! In order to make the material bend in exactly the right place, cut a groove along the bend line.

! Allow the CAM machine a number of cutting passes. Do not try to cut through material in one go.
! Make sure the CAM machine cuts at the right speed for the material.
! Take care when making, do not rush!

Action plan

Use the following steps as the basis of an action plan for manufacturing your product:

Action	Resources	Time needed
1 Fix material to the bed of the CAM machine with double-sided tape	• 3 mm Foamex or acrylic plastic sheet • Double-sided sticky tape	10 mins
2 Fix correct cutting tool into CAM machine	• CAM machine • Allen key	3 mins
3 Set CAM machine to ready	• CAM machine	2 mins
4 Load your design into CAD software and select area for cutting	• PC • CAD software	5 mins
5 Set up cutting depths in CAD software	• PC • CAD software	5 mins
6 **Output** design from CAD software to CAM machine	• PC • CAD software • CAM machine	1 min
7 Watch CAM machine cut material and make product, including engraving	• CAM machine	5 mins
8 Remove cut material from bed	• Ruler	1 min
9 Clean up material	• Ruler or needle files	5 mins
10 Bend product	• Line heater	5 mins
11 Assemble product	• Product • Plastic sucker • Joggly eyes	5 mins
12 Design packaging	• Card, pencils/pens, scissors • Plastic bag	30 mins
13 Test product	• Product	10 mins

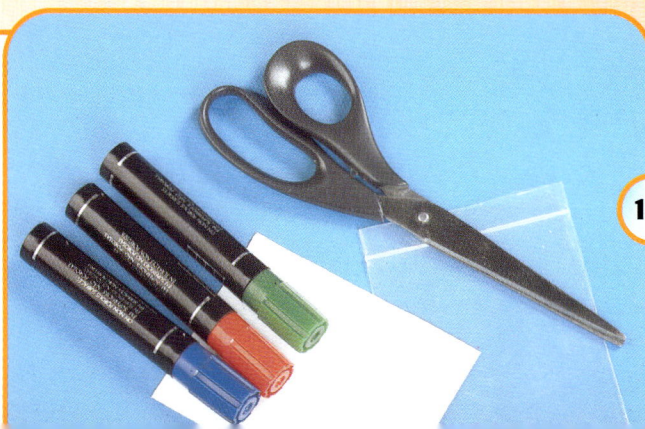

12

1

9

7

Do not put your hands in or near the machine when it is working.

Evaluation

Answer the following questions about your product to help you **evaluate** how your product development went:

- Am I pleased with my finished product?
- In what ways could I make my product better?
- Did I use my time effectively? In what ways?
- Was my design work of a good standard?
- Could my design work be better?
- What do other people think of my work?
- What parts of the project did I find difficult and why?
- Did I enjoy the project?

Project 3: Animal pen

The design brief

A primary school is running a campaign entitled 'Making writing fun'. As part of this project the school has asked you to design and manufacture a range of fun, colourful pens based on an animal theme. The pens must be manufactured using CAD/CAM and use a standard ballpoint cartridge.

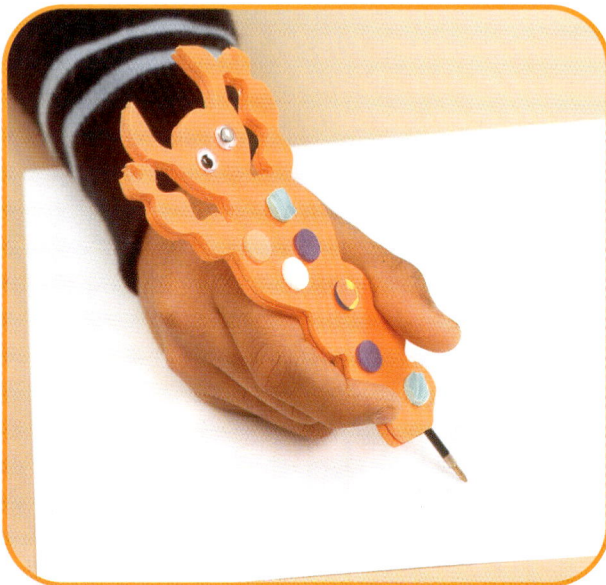

Product specification

The product **specification** is a list of things your product must be or do:

- the product will use a standard ballpoint pen cartridge
- the product will be made from Foamex or acrylic plastic
- the product must have an animal theme
- the maximum size of the product is to be 160 mm x 80 mm
- the product can use joggly eyes up to 8 mm in diameter
- the product must be safe for users and should last and withstand regular use
- the product should be **aesthetically** pleasing.

Research

Before starting work on your project, you should do some product research. Identify and analyse a number of low price ballpoint pens. What is good and bad about each pen? How do you think it could be improved? You should also draw a diagram of the **milling** cutter and calculate how long the groove to hold the pen cartridge needs to be.

Resources

Materials and components

- 3 mm thick plastic – acrylic or Foamex
- flexible neoprene foamed plastic
- double-sided sticky tape
- pen cartridge (inside of a pen, the tip and part that holds the ink)
- pre-manufactured joggly eyes

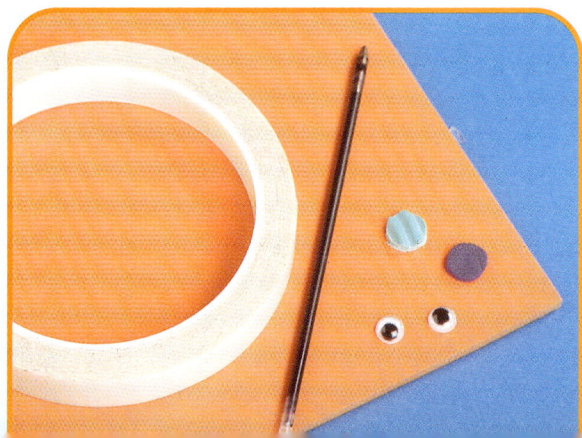

Tools and equipment

- Computer Aided Design software – Techsoft 2D Design Tools® or equivalent
- Computer Aided Manufacture hardware – **CNC** machine with milling and engraving capabilities, for example a Roland EGX-300, Roland Modela MDX-20 or Suregrave Wizzard DT
- scissors, needle files, abrasive paper, ruler, Allen key

Design ideas

1 First, do a quick brainstorm about animals that could form the basis of your design ideas. This can be presented in the form of a bubble or spider diagram.

2 Using a pencil and paper sketch different ideas, for example, animals.

3 Transform your best idea into a silhouetted shape.

4 Using a CAD package, draw your shape onto the computer.

5 Using the CAD software, modify your design idea until you are happy with it.

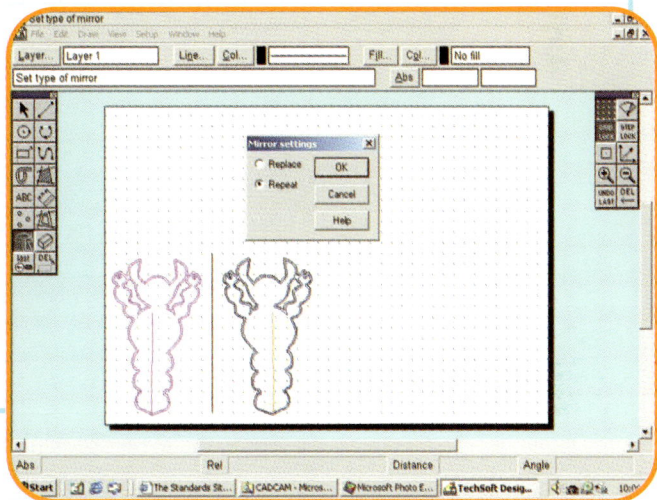

Hints for success

- ! Keep your ideas simple. Some of the best ideas are not complex, but still very effective.
- ! Use **templates** if needed for more complex design details.
- ! Use the full range of drawing tools on the CAD software to manipulate and change your design. In this project, the important thing to get right is the length of the groove which holds the pen cartridge. The actual shape of the holder only needs to be drawn once and then mirrored. Use the transform function to mirror the image down the central axis.
- ! Allow the CAM machine a number of cutting passes. Don't try to cut through material in one go.
- ! Make sure the CAM machine cuts at the right speed for the material.
- ! Always take the time to finish your product with files and abrasive paper.
- ! Take care when making, don't rush!

Action plan

Use the following steps as the basis of an action plan for manufacturing your product:

Action	Resources	Time needed
1 Fix material to the bed of the CAM machine with double-sided tape	• 3 mm Foamex or acrylic plastic sheet • Double-sided sticky tape	10 mins
2 Fix correct cutting tool into CAM machine	• **Milling** or engraving tool • Allen key • CAM machine	3 mins
3 Set CAM machine to ready	• CAM machine	2 mins
4 Load your design into CAD software and select area for cutting	• PC • CAD software	5 mins
5 Set up cutting depths in CAD software	• PC • CAD software	5 mins
6 **Output** design from CAD software to CAM machine	• PC • CAD software • CAM machine	1 min
7 Watch CAM machine cut material and make product	• CAM machine	5 min
8 Remove cut material from bed	• Ruler	1 mins
9 Clean up material with a ruler or needle files	• Ruler (for acrylic) or needle files	5 min
10 Insert pen cartridge and stick two halves together. Attach decoration to finished product	• Double-sided sticky tape • Pen cartridge • Joggly eyes	10 mins
11 Test product	• Product	10 mins

10

2

4

9

Evaluation

Answer the following questions about your product
to help you to **evaluate** how your product development went:

- Am I pleased with my finished product?
- In what ways could I make my product better?
- Did I use my time effectively? In what ways?
- Was my design work of a good standard?
- Could my design work be better?
- What do other people think of my work?
- What parts of the project did I find difficult and why?
- Did I enjoy the project?

Project 4:
Funky soap – FOAP!

The design brief

You have been asked to design and manufacture a new novelty soap product using CAD/CAM. The soap must be **machined** using TS foam, a material highly suited to 3D machining. This can then be used as a **former** for the **vacuum forming** process. Soap granules can then be melted and poured into the mould. The packaging of the product is very important, and you will need to develop this area fully.

Product specification

This is a list of all of the things that your soap must have or do:

- the product must be developed using an appropriate 3D CAD software package such as Pro/Desktop®. (The final product must be presented as a **third angle orthographic drawing** and as a fully **rendered** image.)
- the maximum dimensions of the product are 50 mm x 50 mm x 20 mm
- the initial form must be machined from Pro/Desktop® using appropriate CAM equipment, for example the Roland Modela MDX-20, using TS foam or equivalent
- the mould must be vacuum formed using 0.5 mm polystyrene sheet
- the soap granules can be coloured and scented as required.

Research

You should think about how solid soap products are packaged, and what scent and colours you are going to use to help you develop your product. Try looking around shops or at catalogues or on the Internet as part of your research.

Resources

Materials and components

- 50 mm x 50 mm x 30 mm TS foam block
- 0.5 mm polystyrene sheet for vacuum forming
- soap granules
- colours and scents for soap
- resealable plastic bag
- thin card to make package insert

Tools and equipment

- 3D CAD software such as Pro/Desktop®
- Roland Modela MDX-20 (or the MDX-15) for 3D manufacture
- milling machine, cutter
- heating source such as a stove or microwave oven and a suitable container for the soap
- access to the Internet, PC and printer
- double-sided sticky tape
- knife
- vacuum forming machine

Design ideas

1 Design a range of ideas that satisfy the requirements learned from your research and the **specifications**. Try to keep your ideas simple, and use a theme if possible.

2 Choose the idea that you think is best and draw it on a CAD software package.

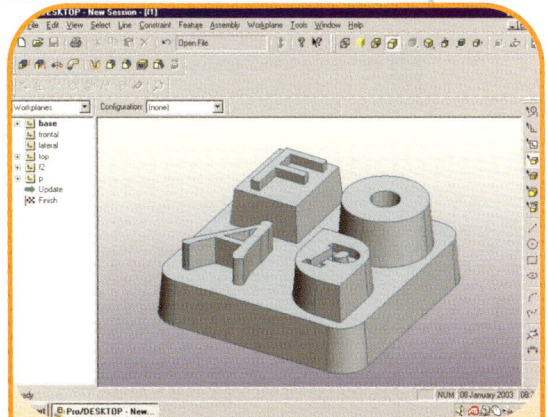

The FOAP design set up on the CAD software ready for manufacturing.

Hints for success

! Your chosen design solution should be the most effective of your design ideas. Try to keep it simple, as this will make it easier to transfer into the CAD software.

! Put a chamfer (a cutaway or sloping edge) on the sides of the shape. This will make it easier to withdraw the former from the mould after it has been vacuum formed.

! Once you have designed your soap in Pro/Desktop® you must export it as a STL file. This is a file that the CAM machine will understand. The machine's software will then calculate how to make the product.

Action plan

Use the following steps as the basis of an action plan for manufacturing your product:

Action	Resources	Time needed
1 Export your Pro/Desktop file as a STL file into the CAM machine software	• CAM software	10 mins
2 Fix material to the bed of the CAM machine with double-sided tape	• Double-sided sticky tape, TS foam	5 mins
3 Fix correct cutting tool into CAM machine	• 3D CAM machine • **Milling** machine, cutter	5 mins
4 Set CAM machine to ready	• CAM machine	1 min
5 Model the machining process on the software to make sure that is going to work properly	• CAM software	5 mins
6 Ensure that the machine is safe. Start cutting	• CAM machine	30 mins

> **Health and Safety:** Watch the whole of the machining process throughout. Be ready to stop the machine if anything goes wrong.

Action	Resources	Time needed
7 Place TS foam shape in **vacuum forming** machine and make a mould out of 0.5 mm polystyrene	• TS foam shape • Vacuum forming machine • 0.5 mm polystyrene sheet	5 mins

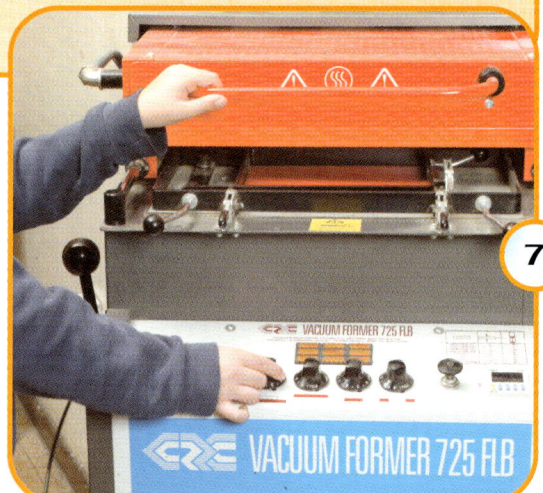

5

7

Action	Resources	Time needed

Action	Resources	Time needed
8 Heat the soap granules to 40°C in a container on a stove or in a microwave. Once the soap is liquefied and clear, add colour and scent and stir	• Soap granules • Scents • Colours • Container • Stove or microwave oven	5 mins
9 Pour soap into mould and allow to cool and set	• Vacuum formed mould	30 mins
10 Remove soap from mould	• Knife	10 mins
11 Create the packaging for the soap. The soap requires an airtight container – a resealable plastic bag is ideal	• Plastic bag • Card for insert • Paper and pencils • Printer	1 hour
12 Test product	• Product	10 mins

8

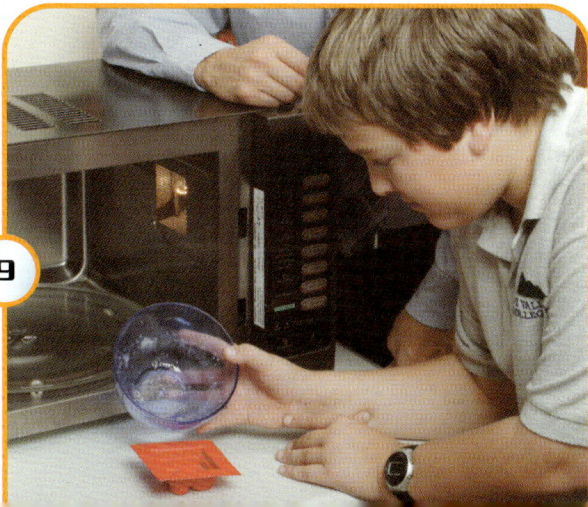

9

Evaluation

Answer the following questions about your product to help you **evaluate** how your product development went:

- Does the soap satisfy the requirements of the specification?
- Am I pleased with my finished product?
- What parts of the project did I find difficult and why?
- Was my design work of a good standard?
- Could my design work be better?
- What do other people think of my work?
- Did I enjoy the project?
- In what ways could I make my product better?

Mini projects

Here are some ideas for mini projects that you can make. The manufacturing time is short and the projects do not need many materials.

1: Bookmark

The design brief

Design and manufacture a **prototype** for a bookmark that could be used by children.

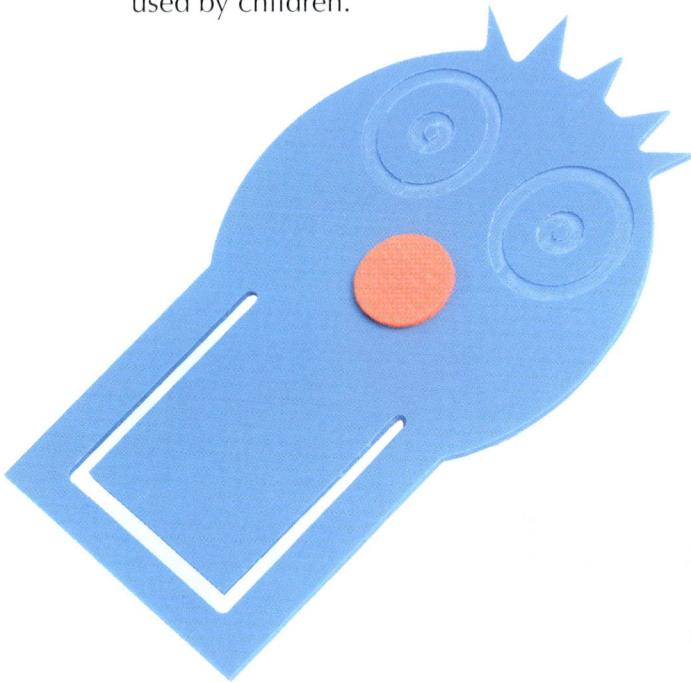

Product specification

This is a list of all of the things that your bookmark must have or do:

- the product must be manufactured using 1 mm thick polystyrene
- the maximum size of the product is 150 mm x 100 mm
- it must be possible to secure the product to a page in a book without damaging the paper
- the bookmark must appeal to children.

Resources

- 1 mm thick polystyrene sheet
- CAD program
- CAD hardware – **CNC** machine with **milling** and engraving capabilities, such as a Roland EGX-300 or Modela MDX-20, or the Suregrave Wizzard DT

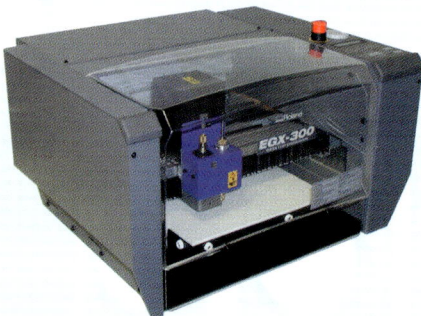

2: Fridge magnet

The design brief

Design and manufacture a fridge magnet that will show children how to spell the names of different animals or objects.

Product specification

This is a list of all of the things that your fridge magnet must have or do:

* the product must be manufactured using 3 mm Foamex
* the maximum size of the product is 60 mm x 60 mm
* the product must use a piece of magnetic sticky-backed tape for attaching to the fridge door
* the product must be safe for all users
* the product should last and withstand reasonable use
* the product should be **aesthetically** pleasing.

Resources

* 3 mm thick Foamex sheet
* CAD program
* CAD hardware – CNC machine with milling and engraving capabilities, such as a Roland EGX-300, Roland Modela MDX-20, Suregrave or Wizzard DT
* pre-manufactured joggly eyes
* magnetic tape

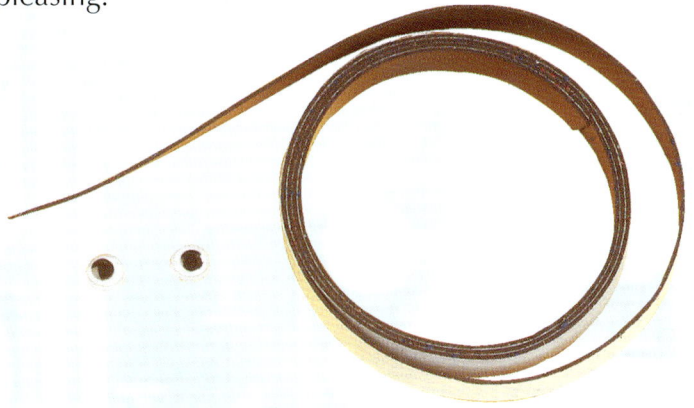

The design brief

Design and manufacture a slot-together toy using CAD/CAM technologies. The animal must be packaged safely with clear instructions about how it is assembled.

Product specification

This is a list of all of the things that your toy must have or do:

- the product must be manufactured using 3mm Foamex
- the maximum size of the product is 150 mm x 150 mm
- the product must be packaged in a 190 mm x 190 mm plastic bag
- the product must be safe for all users
- the product should be able to withstand reasonable use
- the product should be **aesthetically** pleasing.

Resources

- 3 mm thick Foamex sheet
- CAD program
- CAM hardware – **CNC** machine with **milling** and engraving capabilities, such as a Roland EGX-300, Roland Modela MDX-20 or Suregrave Wizzard DT
- pre-manufactured joggly eyes
- 190 mm x 190 mm resealable plastic bags
- card for instructions.

4: Ball-bearing game

The design brief

Design and manufacture a travel game that could be used on long journeys. The game must use a ball-bearing and a maze.

Product specification

This is a list of all of the things that your game must have or do:

- the product will be made from 3 mm acrylic plastic
- the product will be sandwiched by clear acrylic
- the maximum size of the product is A6 (15 cm x 10.5 cm) – hand-held size
- the product will use a maze
- the product must be safe for all users
- the product should be able to withstand reasonable use
- the product should be aesthetically pleasing.

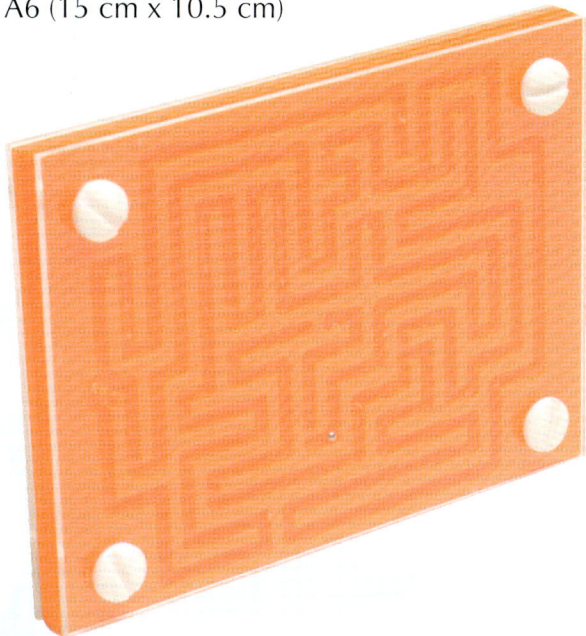

Resources

- acrylic, clear, 3 mm
- acrylic, coloured, 3 mm
- CAD software
- ball-bearing, 2 mm
- rapid assembly 6 mm nylon post and slotted screws
- CNC CAM hardware – CNC machine with milling and engraving capabilities, such as a Roland EGX-300, Modela MDX-20 or Suregrave Wizzard DT
- ball nose tool milling bit, 3 mm

Glossary

aesthetics what something looks and feels like

analysis examining facts that you have gathered together about something and then thinking about them

casting heating a solid until it becomes liquid and then pouring it into a hard mould. When cooled, the material can be removed from the mould.

CNC Computer Numeric Control

commission pay another company to design or manufacture a product

components parts of a product

compression switch switch that is turned on and off by something pressing on it

computer model digital version of a product that is created on a computer before being manufactured using the computer information

consumer anybody who uses a product

contouring line placed around a drawing to take into account the diameter of the cutting tool

controlled experiment experiment done under specific conditions

criteria various standards set on which you can make a judgement about something

design brief statement that describes what a product is required to be like and do

detailing CAD solid modelling CAD software used to develop the manufacturing detail of the product

ergonomics how products and places are designed to be efficient for people to use

evaluate/evaluation comparing the finished product with the specification

fabrication manufacturing something from different materials

flowchart series of linked boxes that show the order of making something or a control system

former shape around which a mould can be produced

injection moulding common industrial process where plastic granules are heated to become fluid then injected into a mould

lathe machine that can cut and shape round materials

laser etching use of laser technology to cut and shape materials

machined something that has been cut by a machine

market research studying what consumers want and like, and fashion trends

milling/milling machine machine that has a horizontal bed and vertical cutter

modelling using a computer to generate products, versions of or making small-scale ideas

non-ferrous metal metals that do not contain iron

output sending information, such as an image, from a computer, usually to a CAM machine

override process of stopping or changing a CNC machine that is already running a program

plotter machine that draws designs on paper based on comments from a computer. Plotters differ from printers in that they use pens to draw lines.

proportion correct relation of different parts to each other, which look pleasing when put together

prototype first version of a product, used for pre-production testing

rapid prototyping rapid prototyping uses advanced technologies such as stereolithography to make 3D models quickly and cheaply for pre-production testing

rendered drawn or presented with colour and texture

specification set of criteria that the final solution or finished product must achieve

stereolithography (SLA) method used in rapid modelling or prototyping. A stereolithography machine uses a computer-controlled laser to create a 3D part. It does this by exposing liquid plastic in a tank and hardening it.

target market type or group of people or companies that a product is aimed at

template standard CAD file that can be used as a basis for design work

third angle orthographic drawing type of technical drawing that shows an object from three viewpoints, called projections

tolerance acceptable amount of error or inaccuracy

undercut to cut away a part below or under a thing

vacuum forming method of moulding plastics over a shape called a former. The plastic is heated until soft, then sucked over a hard former.

visualization CAD use of surface modelling CAD software to show the outside shape, colour and texture of the product

Resources

The following websites will be useful to look at when sourcing materials and making the projects in the book:

www.ame-solutions.com – the AME company website

www.designtechnology.org.uk – a website created by the authors, dedicated to D&T education. It contains worksheets and project ideas.

www.roland.co.uk – the Roland company website

www.suregrave.com – the Suregrave company website

www.techsoft.co.uk – the Techsoft company website

Index

Titles in the *Practical Design & Technology* series are:

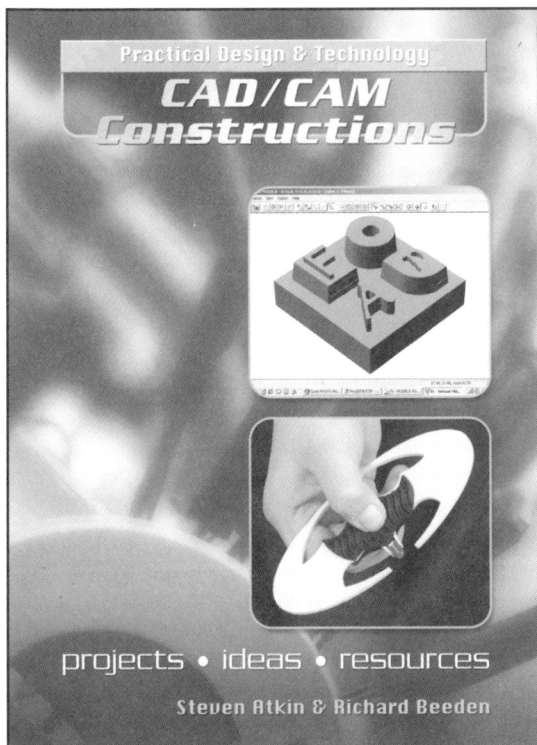

Practical Design & Technology
CAD/CAM Constructions
projects • ideas • resources
Steven Atkin & Richard Beeden

Hardback   0 431 17582 9

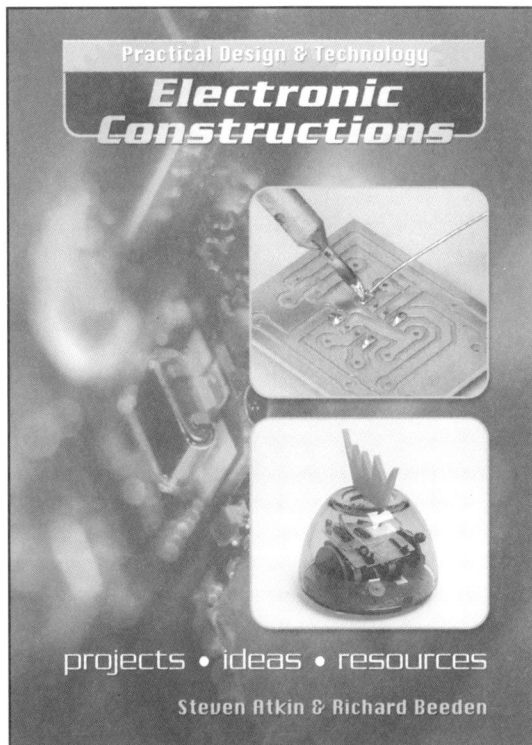

Practical Design & Technology
Electronic Constructions
projects • ideas • resources
Steven Atkin & Richard Beeden

Hardback   0 431 17580 2

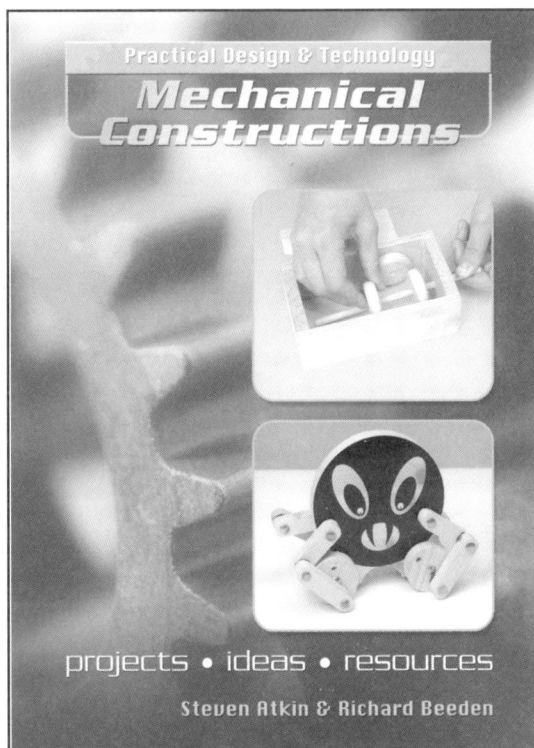

Practical Design & Technology
Mechanical Constructions
projects • ideas • resources
Steven Atkin & Richard Beeden

Hardback   0 431 17581 0

Find out about the other titles in this series on our website www.heinemann.co.uk/library